Milton Keynes UK
Ingram Content Group UK Ltd.
UKHW011313220324
439969UK00008B/12

MEMOIR,
ETC.

To the philosopher, the philanthropist, the physiologist—to the man interested in the whole human family, and capable of drawing liberal conclusions from the various characteristics which, under different aspects, it exhibits, this brief memoir of one who stands forth a conspicuous specimen of a " distinct " and " marked " race, and a living illustration of their intellectual capabilities, will be peculiarly acceptable.

It will tell of an Ethiopian—" a black "—who, notwithstanding the abject state in which most of his kind

"Live, and move, and have their being,"

has obtained, and maintains among us Europeans—" whites "—who deem ourselves to be the most civilized and enlightened people upon God's earth, a reputation whose acquisition demands the highest qualities of the mind and the noblest endowments of the person.

The acquirements of a scholar, the conception of a poet, and the accomplishments of a gentleman, must be united in one individual before he can become eminent as an actor. These mental and physical advantages have been found to exist in an African; and to such a degree are they by him exhibited, that he, in his single person, and as a champion of his sable brethren, gives the lie direct to the most " refined " among us who, in his prejudice, his exclusiveness, and his ignorance, shall harbour the remotest doubt of an African being, to all intents and purposes,

" A man and a brother."

It is not, however, the present endeavour of the writer to "point a moral and adorn a tale ;" but to give, in the fewest possible words, a concise history of one whose career, describe it as you may, cannot fail to fill the reflective mind with thoughts of deepest interest. It is impossible to regard one man of colour as a being of extraordinary faculties, possessing a soul capable of appreciating, and endowments equal to the representation of immortal Shakespeare's great creations, and not sigh in serious contemplation of the wrongs of thousands of his countrymen, treated by their paler brethren as mindless, heartless, soulless, feelingless clay, bearing the corporeal impress of humanity, but cruelly or thoughtlessly denied its spiritual attributes. No: a moral lesson *will* present, and even intrude itself with the simple fact, that the swarthy native of Africa is as capable of cultivation as the fairest son of Albion : a fact in which the better portion of mankind rejoice, and one from which the advocate of slavery turns, but turns in vain, for Truth must in time prevail.

Mr. Ira Aldridge, the gentleman whose memoir is here given, has been long celebrated in the provinces, and not altogether unknown in London, as a performer of surpassing excellence. His fame as an actor has extended far and wide throughout Great Britain, but not until now has the Metropolis become perfectly acquainted with his singular merits. His recent appearance at the Surrey Theatre has created not only a sensation in the theatrical world, but a degree of curiosity throughout society in general; and the novelty of his performances, and his unequivocal success, are matters so striking and suggestive, that a brief account of his origin and professional progress, requires no apologetic preface; and we verily believe that the Anti-Slavery Society have not published a tract containing more incontrovertible evidence of the African's natural claims, than may be found in these pages.

Well-informed people need not be told that a great amount of the highest order of human intelligence is to be met with in people of colour. We have Africans who have attained eminence in the arts and sciences. In the Church, the Law, and in Medicine—in all our professions and trades, have they won honours and wealth; and the hue of the skin is known to be no natural impediment to the acquirement of learning, the cultivation of ingenuity, and the practice of virtue; but Mr. Aldridge is, we believe, the first born negro who has earned for himself a reputation in the highest walks of the Drama, and he deserves all the credit of having so signalized himself.

We cannot pay to the inky-visaged children of the Sun those personal compliments which are often lavished upon fairer faces. There is black marble as well as white; but those varied tints which captivate the eye—the beauties of colour—that are not even "skin deep," and such as the rose, the lily, the violet, and other flowers display, are peculiar to European countenances. The "pure red and white," however, even in contrast to the blackness with which the Devil is painted, what are they in reality to the scientific and philosophic observer?—what are they in the eye of our common Creator? With such disadvantages as strongest prejudice can create, and generous natures cannot entirely overcome, it is no small triumph to Mr. Aldridge that the following lines have been addressed to him by one of our countrywomen who, in a spirit liberal and commendable, has availed herself of language which, we think, no impartial witness of the African's performances can say is misapplied :—

> " Thine is the spell o'er hearts
> Which only Acting lends ;
> The youngest of the Sister Arts,
> There all their beauty blends :
> For ill can Poetry express
> Full many a tone of thought sublime,
> And Painting, mute and motionless,
> Steals but a glance of time.
> But by the mighty Actor brought,
> Illusion's perfect triumph 's come :
> Verse ceases to be airy thought
> And Sculpture to be dumb."

Ridicule, that powerful weapon even in the hands of fools, assails those who wear

" The shadowed livery of the burnished Sun,"

more than all the other sons of man upon the face of the globe. It immortal part of man he described what was universal. But fancy a black Juliet! And why not? May there not be an Ethiopian Juliet to an Ethiopian Romeo? So reasoned and so *felt* the coloured members of the amateur corps, when Mr. Aldridge undertook to perform the love-sick swain in a sable countenance. Certain Yankees, with a degree of illiberality peculiar to *some* "Liberals," had no notion of such indulgences being allowed to "niggers," whose "tarnation conceit and considerable effrontery licked natur slick outright." One Stephen Price, a manager of some repute, became actually *jealous* of the success of the "real Ethiopians," and emissaries were employed to put them down. They attracted considerable notice; and people who went to ridicule, remained to admire, albeit there must have been ample scope for the suggestion of the ridiculous. Riots ensued, and destruction fell upon the little theatre. Of course there was no protection or redress to be obtained from the magistracy (for, unhappily, they were whites), and the company dissolved, much to the chagrin of the Juliet elect, who declared that *nothing but* envy prevented the blacks from putting the whites completely out of countenance.

It was about this time that the celebrated and inimitable mimic and comedian, Mr. Mathews, was on a tour through the United States, from which he brought materials for making many a night "At Home," before an Adelphi audience. He chanced to see Mr. Aldridge on the stage, and made the most of what he saw. The African Roscius thus, at a public dinner in this country, gave his version of the story :—

"Mr. Mathews paid a visit to the theatre on one of the evenings of my performance, and this occurrence he has made the vehicle for one of the most amusing anecdotes in his well known 'Trip to America.' There is certainly a good deal more in the manner of his telling the story, than in the matter, and he has embellished the whole circumstance with a great many fictitious variations, not the less amusing because untrue, but which are pardonable enough in such a work as Mr. Mathews's, the materials of which are acknowledged to have been made up as much of fiction as of truth. He says that on the occasion alluded to I played Hamlet, and in the celebrated soliloquy, 'To be, or not to be,' on my coming to the passage 'and by opposing end them,' the similarity of the sound of the words reminding the audience of the negro melody of 'Oppossum up a gum tree,' they loudly called for it, and the polite request Mr. Mathews makes me accede to in the following elegant language :—'Well den, ladies and gemmen, you like Oppossum up a gum tree better den you like Hamlet? me sing him to you;' which I, according to the anecdote, did three or four times, much to the exquisite edification of my black hearers, and then resumed my part of the pensive prince. The truth, however, is, that I never attempted the character of Hamlet in my life, and I need not say that the whole of the ludicrous scene so well and so humorously described by Mr. Mathews, never occurred at all."

Mr. Aldridge was bent upon witnessing the performances which took place in the country of his father's adoption, and opportunities for so doing presented themselves under the following, to him fortuitous, circumstances:—

He had a school-fellow who was in the habit of taking Mr. Henry Wallack's dresses to the Chatham Theatre, and the acquaintance of this boy he assiduously cultivated. With a little contrivance and the assistance of this privileged individual, young Aldridge obtained an introduction to the mysteries of the Stage. The boy soon after died of the yellow fever, and the coloured aspirant eagerly tendered his services, and obtained the wished-for *entrée* to "behind the scenes," by becoming the bearer of the leading actor's dresses, and making himself generally useful in the way of running to and fro. This employment, if known to his father, was not that in which he wished to see his son engaged; but amply was that son repaid for his services, by being permitted to gaze upon the scenes which presented themselves.

It has been said by goodnatured people who rejoice in distorting facts to the prejudice of those to whom they can be disadvantageously applied, that Mr. Aldridge, when a youth, was the errand-boy of Mr. H. Wallack, and in that capacity picked up whatever theatrical knowledge he acquired. There is no doubt but he availed himself as much as possible of whatever lessons fell in his way, and the greatest actor of any age must have done something of the kind; with this difference, that others had less difficulty in obtaining instruction. Young Aldridge derived no pecuniary profit from his services, but was too happy to render them in exchange for the delight he experienced in gaining admission to the precincts of what he most admired. There the young Roscius hung about the "wings," receiving intoxicating pleasure, listening with rapture to the wildest rant, and strengthening his hopes of emulating the most admired actors who presented themselves. But a sudden termination was put to his nightly enjoyment; through the interest of Bishops Brenton and Milner, he was entered at Schenectady College, near New York, in order to prepare himself for the ministry; and here for awhile he entered into theological studies. Notwithstanding the progress he made in learning, he lacked advancement in his religious profession. No qualities of the mind could compensate in the eyes of Americans for the dark hue of his skin; the prevailing prejudice, so strong among all classes, was against him, and it was deemed advisable to send him to Great Britain. He was accordingly shipped for the Old Country, and entered at the Glasgow University, where, under Professor Sandford, he obtained several premiums and the medal for Latin composition.

Here he remained about eighteen months, when he broke entirely from the scholastic thraldom imposed upon him.

Even religious pursuits could not damp his ardour for the Stage. His early preference "grew with his growth and strengthened with his strength;" and while yet young he started for England, determined to make an attempt to appear in public before an audience who, whatever the severity of their criticism, he believed, would not condemn him on account of colour.

It was in the year 1825 the African Roscius came to England—the Old Mother Country whom he had so often heard reviled in the New World, but to which, in common with every American (whatever they may affect to the contrary), he looked with respect and deeply-rooted interest: feelings more or less disguised and suppressed among the free and enlightened Yankees, as men are wont to hide what does not agree with their vanity. He brought with him no transatlantic recommendations. An actor of colour was a novelty in this country not tolerated in that. Here we have distinctions without differences—there they have no distinctions but differences that are exceedingly great. "Without a friend," we are told, "the world is but a wilderness." There is much truth in the saying, for whatever our station, we are never wholly independent of one another in a social community. A man, nevertheless, may be his own friend to a very great extent, and Mr. Aldridge found that he had few others than himself to rely upon. He brought with him, however, a letter of introduction from Mr. Henry Wallack, whose knowledge of him and his character has been already alluded to. He had now to hammer his way into the theatrical world, and sought an opening for applying "the wedge." A very small aperture presented itself, but that was enough, for, as in rending timber, all depends upon the power and skill that are applied to the opening; and public opinion, however hard and stubborn, seldom fails to yield to the force of merit, provided it be properly and perseveringly brought into action.

Mr. Aldridge commenced at the Royalty, at the East End, under the management of Mr. Dunn, where he first felt the British pulse, and found it favourable to his pretensions. This was in 1826, soon after his arrival from Glasgow.

He made his *debut* as Othello, in which he was highly successful. Thus encouraged and strengthened he procured an engagement at the Cobourg, where Messrs. Leclerc, Davidge, Hornblower, and Bengough, were the managers; here he played Oroonoko, Gambia, Zarambo, and or two characters, and obtained great applause.

While there, he entered into an engagement—a solemn one, which, when once made, is peculiarly and particularly binding on both sides—he entered "the holy bonds of matrimony," and undertook to perform the part of a good husband for the rest of his life, to an English lady of respectability and superior accomplishments. The manner in which the match came about has a dash of romance in it, and may be thus briefly told.

Mr. Aldridge, after performing Gambia, in "The Slave," was invited by a friend to visit a private box, to receive the congratulations of a party who had witnessed his acting, and, from the interest he had excited in their minds, had expressed a desire to see the hero of the play in *propria persona*. The actor was formally introduced, and in that short interview commenced an intimacy which, six weeks after, ended in his marriage with a lady who was present, the ~~natural~~ daughter of a member of Parliament, and a man of high standing in the county of Berks. The lady played, to some extent, a modern Desdemona to Mr. Aldridge's Othello, for he unexpectedly had the power to say, in reply to relations—

> That I have ta'en away this old man's daughter,
> It is most true; true I have married her.

He was not accused of using "drugs, charms, conjuration, or mighty magic," in obtaining the lady whose affections came to him—

> ——— By request and such fair question
> As soul to soul affordeth.

But her father was much after Brabantio's way of thinking. His eyes mental and physical were not like those of the Duke, who said:—

> If virtue no delighted beauty lack,
> Your son-in-law is far more fair than black.

Mrs. Aldridge "saw her husband's visage in his mind," and that, we can venture to say, if it has changed at all, has improved by time and trial. Ever since her marriage she has accompanied her husband upon his professional journeys, and his theatrical campaign has been a long one, for there is no British town containing a respectable theatre which has not been crowded to witness his mimic art.

Thence Mr. Aldridge went to Sadlers' Wells, where he performed for a few nights in several leading parts; and next to the Olympic. Thus he modestly and hesitatingly, as it were, edged himself in, tremblingly alive to the prejudice with which he had previously had to contend—a prejudice to which, indeed, he had from infancy been taught to *submit*, however keenly he felt its influence and however plainly he saw its cruel injustice. But he was young; and a genial soil and atmosphere soon causes a sapling tree to take root and spread forth its branches. He had found the true Land of Liberty, and he saw a fair prospect of prospering in it. Having, one may say, felt his way thus far in comparative obscurity, he withdrew into the provinces, the better to fit himself for a greater trial in the metropolis. He accordingly took a country tour, acting in succession at Brighton, Chichester, Leicester, Liverpool, Manchester, Glasgow, Edinburgh, Exeter, Belfast, and so on, returning to London after a lapse of seven years, an apprenticeship which he had turned to good account. During this time Mr. Aldridge had studied deeply and laboured hard at his profession. In every provincial town that he had visited his reception had been flattering in the extreme; and his fame as a country actor, as is generally the case in such instances, had reached the capital.

Notwithstanding the favourable impression "The African Kean," as he was then termed, made wherever he appeared, he repeatedly failed in procuring an engagement at Dublin. Mr. Calcraft, the spirited and accomplished manager of the Theatre Royal, could not be prevailed upon by letter to accept the services of the man of colour, at a venture: there was "something so absurd about it." Mr. Aldridge, therefore, went there at his own cost, and had an interview with the manager. The result was favourable to his ambition, and he was engaged "for a limited number of nights," as the saying goes, establishing a popularity which has never since abated.

Edmund Kean had been previously secured to appear at this theatre; and the management endeavoured to dissuade Mr. Aldridge from taking the part of Othello, as the celebrated tragedian was known to complain if his favourite characters were played just previously to his acting them himself. Mr. Aldridge was urged to come forward as Zanga, but he persisted in playing Othello, and had his way. He performed as Othello in December, 1831, and made a great hit. The Dublin people were surprised and delighted. His "sable suit" gave him additional interest in the eyes of the warm-hearted Hibernians, and the newspapers spoke in glowing terms of his rare abilities. This was the first hold that he took upon the British public, because his first appearance before an important tribunal belonging to it. He subsequently ran through his list of favourite characters, viz.: Zanga, Rolla, Gambia, Alhambra, Mungo, &c., in all of which he gained enthusiastic applause. From the many favourable critiques which appeared at the time, we will only quote the following, which by no means contains the greatest amount of praise :—

Mr. Aldridge's first appearance was in a character in every respect suited to his genius, and most strongly calculated to draw forth those extraordinary powers, of which this actor is so distinguished a master. In all those parts where Desdemona calls into action on the part of the noble-minded Moor the softer and finer feelings of the heart, as, for instance, when she pleads for the restoration of Cassio, his responses were delivered in a manner so chaste, tender, and affectionate, that they were deeply felt by the whole audience. Many of those passages expressive of the finer feelings of our nature were most beautifully delivered in a softly subdued tone of voice, which was remarkable for its clearness and distinctness of tone. It was not, however, until Iago had roused his mind to jealousy that the actor became truly terrible and sublime. Beautifully and appropriately as were the softer feelings displayed and expressed, it was in the expression of the strong passions of jealousy and revenge that were raging in the bosom of the distracted Moor that Mr. Aldridge rose to a degree of excellence that we have never seen surpassed, albeit that we have seen the first of his contemporaries in the same character. When Iago began to pour his domestic poison into the ears of Othello, and he became alternately jealous of Desdemona's virtue and doubtful of Iago's honesty, his bursts of feeling, succeeded by fierce ebullitions of passion, were at once masterly, grand, and peculiar; and when in the agony of his soul, he gave vent to the passage,
"Who doats, yet doubts;
Suspects, yet strongly loves,"

there was not one solitary individual amongst the audience whose heart did not feel, and whose hands did not applaud to the very echo, the soul-stirring eloquence with which the passage was delivered, whilst the dark and broad features of the actor presented to all who beheld them a faithful index of the contending passions which had placed his soul upon the rack. His seizure of Iago, when he seeks to extort from him some proof of Desdemona's dishonesty was also quite original, and well executed. Indeed, his entire representation of Othello is a masterly performance, as cleverly executed as it is originally conceived, and one which will never fail to convince any intelligent audience that the actor possesses a genius not unworthy of the fame he has acquired.

Edmund Kean came to Dublin while the African was there and saw him act, upon which, with the goodnature conspicuous in all he did, he gave him a letter of recommendation to the manager of the Bath Theatre, to the following effect:—

"Dublin, January 3, 1832.

"Dear Bellamy,—I beg to introduce to your notice Mr. Aldridge, the African Roscius, whose performances I have witnessed with great pleasure. He possesses wondrous versatility, and I am sure, under your judicious generalship, will prove a card in Bath. I have not yet recovered from the fatigues of my journey, but hope to be myself in a day or two.

"I remain, dear Bellamy, truly yours, "E. KEAN."

Upon referring to the playbills of the day, we find that which was issued for Mr. Aldridge's benefit, on Wednesday, December 21, 1831, contains this heading:—

"The African Roscius having been received by the Dublin Audience on each evening of his performance with enthusiastic applause, will ever feel most grateful for the honour conferred upon him, and considers the approbation of the Irish Public as one of the proudest and most distinguished testimonies which has ever been bestowed upon his professional exertions."

Upon this occasion he performed Gambia, in "The Slave," and Mungo, in "The Padlock;" and, in the latter character, he introduced, "by particular desire," the comic nigger song of "Oppossum up a Gum-tree."

At Bath Mr. Aldridge was, if possible, more successful than in Dublin. It is, however, unnecessary to follow his every footstep from town to town during his continued successes. At Belfast Charles Kean played Iago to his Othello, and he Aboan to Charles Kean's Oroonoko. Sheridan Knowles was among those who at that period complimented and encouraged the "only actor of colour upon the Stage." And the testimonials and letters of congratulation and approval which he then received would fill a book, while provincial criticism was uniformly in his favour. We may here extract from a paper a specimen of the general tone of reviews which his acting elicited:—

"Our theatrical campaign opened on Monday evening, with every promise of success, as it introduced to a Wexford audience the celebrated African Roscius, Mr. Aldridge, who appeared as Zanga, in Young's celebrated tragedy of 'The Revenge.' We cannot, indeed, find language sufficiently strong to do justice to this inimitable actor. His opening scene was powerful and affecting, and at once proved to his admiring auditory his just conception of the difficult character he had to sustain. In the third act, when he worked up Alonzo to the assassination of his friend, Don Carlos, by planting in his heart the seeds of jealousy, the manner in which he delivered the few lines, ending with 'to tread upon the Greek and Roman names,' was electrical; and in the last act, where he had completely wrought his victim to his fiendish and hellish purpose, in order to satiate his revenge; and saw Alonzo prostrate—his hellish joy—the self-satisfaction at the wish of destruction he caused—bespoke at once the genius of this mighty actor. During the whole of the last scene there was a breathless silence in the house—so anxious was every one to hear every word he uttered, and pay that respect which transcendent merit deserves. This gentleman is tall in stature, stoutly built, with a strong caste of face of the African mould; his action is most graceful and becoming; his pronunciation clear and distinct, with a deep and mellow tone of voice; in short, Nature has stamped this man as an actor of the first order. The other characters of the play were most respectably sustained by the company. The evening's entertainments concluded with the farce of 'The Padlock:' the part of Mungo by the African Roscius. Here again did we experience a new scene of delight upon his impersonation of this character. If the author of the piece were alive, and after seeing our hero in it, he would say—'that is the man for whom I wrote the piece.' Suffice it to say, he is the first Mungo in the British dominions. The only way to appreciate the character of this man, and to estimate his towering genius, is to go to the theatre and see him. Our old and respected favourite, Mr. J. W. Potter, who is the manager, deserves well of the Wexford people for introducing to them this celebrated character—we trust he will be well repaid for his exertion by full attendance at the theatre during his stay."

The following season Mr. Aldridge returned to Dublin, and, after going through his limited round of characters, acted in a translation of Schiller's "Fiesco," by General D'Aguillar, which had a good run.

The following is a notice relating to him, which appeared in *Saunders' Dublin News Letter*, January 12, 1833:—

"THEATRE-ROYAL.—Last night, Young's tragedy of 'The Revenge' was performed, and the African Roscius played Zanga with a degree of native force and spirit-stirring fidelity that might have made

'Afric and her hundred thrones rejoice,'

could they have beheld their princely representative: his dark features are gifted with an expression that peculiarly fits him for the personation of characters like Zanga, with whose existence all the stronger and darker passions are so closely interwoven, and who are so well described as

'Souls touched with fires, and children of the sun,
With whom revenge is virtue'—

an expression, savage, perhaps, in its origin, and its fiery development, yet conveying sentiments and sensations with a power that 'Europe and her pallid sons' in vain attempt to equal."

At this time M. Laporte, the lessee of the Italian Opera House and Covent Garden, made the African Roscius an offer, which he accepted. His opening was fixed for Wednesday, April 10, 1833; and, after adding to his laurels at Edinburgh, where he played Shylock among other characters, on that night he made his bow for the first time upon the boards of the great "patent theatre," Covent Garden. The *Standard* of April 14, 1833, thus alludes to the circumstance:—

"THEATRE-ROYAL, COVENT GARDEN.—We made a point of being present, for the last three evenings, to witness the performance of that singularly-gifted actor, the African Roscius, who is the first performer of colour that ever appeared on the boards of any theatre in Britain. He had chosen the part of Othello for his first appearance—an undertaking which at present was most hazardous; but, notwithstanding the impression which the inimitable Kean has created in this character, and the genius by which he has made it peculiarly his own, the result showed that the African Roscius was fully justified in making the bold attempt. We at once gladly express our unqualified delight with his delineation of this masterpiece of the divine Shakspere. To attempt a minute description would be as superfluous as difficult; he succeeded in deeply affecting the feelings of his audience, and the representation all through was watched with an intense stillness, almost approaching to awe. At the conclusion, the African Roscius was called for by the unanimous acclamation of the whole house, who, upon his appearance, rose *en masse* to receive him with bursts of applause, waving of hats, handkerchiefs, &c., &c. The *debutant*, evidently deeply affected, expressed his grateful thanks in a very modest and feeling manner, and retired amidst enthusiastic cheering."

Nothing could have been more complete than his success. But there were circumstances against him, and he lost the immediate benefit to which that success entitled him, whilst others, with only half as much, have prospered. The fact of his having appeared as Othello two successive nights before a London audience is one evidence of his triumph, but it was not lasting. The tide of fortune was in his favour, but not "taken at its flood," and hostile and adverse breezes set in to keep him back. Theatres were not doing well, and the "legitimate" business was particularly low. He performed but four nights at Covent Garden; and then his name was withdrawn from the bills. This sudden and extraordinary termination to what was an unequivocal realization of all that could have been hoped of him, may be variously accounted for. M. Laporte was himself capricious, and a manager's motives, aims, plans, contrivances, impulses, decisions, and arrangements, are all his own. The public can seldom see or comprehend them; and managers are very often at a loss to account to themselves for what they do, while to the looker-on their conduct is, in nine cases out of ten, inexplicable. Certain of the public press—a few individuals—were inimical to the histrionic pretensions of the African. There was but little opportunity for assailing him directly and seriously, for in this country men must give something like a reason for what they say in earnest. Ridicule, however, is within the reach of the most unscrupulous and unthinking, and where it *can* be applied, nothing is more effective. Miss Ellen Tree was the Desdemona of Mr. Aldridge's Othello, and certain admirers of that lady, (who was then unmarried, and, as now, a special favourite), were envious of the Moor's familiarity with her fair face, and ridiculed his privilege. Burnt cork and grease, an imitative and dirty dye, upon a tallowy skin, were, in their fastidious and jaundiced eye, unobjectionable as compared with a veritable and natural hue of our Creator's own painting. Men, who have since grown older, and, if we may judge from their literary pursuits, wiser, took a pleasure in scoffing at "the idea" of "a nigger" filling an intellectual character, and surpassing themselves among others in his delineation of poetry, pathos, and passion. It was "the idea" alone which warped their better taste and judgment, for in reality there was nothing to mock. Had Laporte persisted in his undertaking, Mr. Aldridge would soon have been established as a generally known, popular, and extraordinary actor; but he did nothing of the kind. Prejudices, too, will come even across the great Atlantic.

"Cœlum non animum mutant qui trans mare currunt."

And of this fact Mr. Aldridge has been repeatedly reminded upon coming in contact with actors from the United States. They have been ready to forget the immeasurable distance between themselves and the man of colour, physiologically considering one and the other, and, although engaged to perform minor parts to his more prominent ones, they have had the effrontery to assume the hectoring practised upon "Pompeys" in their own country (a kind of bearing at once contemptibly dictatorial and vulgarly familiar), as though they had luckily fallen upon an object so void of self-respect and self-defence, that they may for once indulge in their nationality with impunity. Mr. Aldridge, however, has been too long admired and patronised in Great Britain, and too long absent from "the country of his early adoption," to submit to or tolerate the slightest Yankeeism of *that* kind. He is perfectly conscious of his own moral and physical powers as compared with those of men who would avail themselves of the mere force of prejudice to "put him down;" and the quiet dignity of manners, gentlemanly address, and deportment of the African, seldom fail to check conduct the very reverse—as is usually the case among men; for, let everybody use his own weapon, and the polished and best-tempered has the advantge, especially in a cool hand.

American actors, and some actors who have been in America, to this very day, scoff at the African

" Because that he is black,"

while they themselves are but little admired for all their whiteness. We can very easily understand the latent animosity and open hostility that one performer feels for and shows to another, according to the circumstances which call forth such sentiments; but we have more difficulty in accounting for the unprovoked, uncharitable, unreasonable, and unjustifiable attacks made upon an individual by educated men whose interests can never clash with his, whose profession teaches liberality, and whose principal boast is strict impartiality. But there are many mysteries as to theatrical criticism that puzzle the uninitiated. Be that as it may, the respectable portion of the press, with one consent, extolled the African Roscius during his exceedingly brief engagement at Covent Garden.

Our hero went straight from Covent Garden to the Surrey Theatre, upon which occasion the following announcement in the playbills heralded his appearance there:—

" Mr. Aldridge, a native of Senegal, and known by the appellation of "The African Roscius!" is engaged at this theatre for two nights; and will have the honour of making his first appearance on Monday next, April 22, in Shakspeare's play of "Othello." N.B.—The circumstance of a man of colour performing Othello, on the British Stage, is, indeed, an epoch in the history of theatricals; and the honour conferred upon him, in being called for last week, at Covent Garden Theatre, after the performance, by the unanimous voice of the audience, to receive their tribute of applause, is as highly creditable to the native talent of the sunny climes of Africa, as to the universal liberality of a British Public."

There he likewise performed Oroonoko, Alambra, in " Paul and Virginia," Mungo, and other characters. His stay at the Surrey Theatre was not long.

Mr. Aldridge then again left London, and with an improved reputation. He had stood the test of a London audience, and had not failed; and his value was enhanced among country managers.

No performer has ever enjoyed more local celebrity than Mr. Aldridge has obtained from the period of his quitting the metropolis to this present period of his return to it. From time to time critiques of his performances, setting forth the excellence of his natural and acquired abilities, have reached London, and his name has become familiar to all who take any interest in theatrical matters. Again and again he visited all the principal towns in the United Kingdom, increasing in popularity wherever he appeared. A file of bills containing his performances, and newspapers containing criticisms upon them, is before us: these are so many repeated evidences of his continuous successes. The one announcing how

The singular novelty of an actor of colour, personating the routine of Moorish and African characters, has rendered the performances of the African Roscius highly attractive in the theatres in which he has appeared; and the mighty plaudits with which he had uniformly been honoured by crowded audiences, evince the estimation in which his talents are held by the public;

and the other, eulogizing his various efforts in such terms as the following, which we take—as the landlady, in the song, took the nose of her guest—

' As a sample for all the rest.'

TIPPERARY THEATRICALS.

THE AFRICAN ROSCIUS AND AMATEURS.

This highly-gifted individual, Mr. Aldridge, the celebrated African Roscius worse feeling which were displayed in certain comments, which, during his previous visit, reflected more upon his race and their Creator than Mr. Aldridge himself, and, on the other hand, the high encomiums that the press bestowed upon him, his appearance at the Surrey this time has been attended with some disappointment. In the first place, the house is itself essentially a veritable "minor," whatever be the performers or performances introduced there. In the second place, the management evinced no spirit in bringing him forward. There were neither advertisements, placards, nor posters, to announce the fact, nor any stir made to circulate it, while those who "supported him" ranted so as to mar one moment the interest excited by Mr. Aldridge in another. Yet his usual share of commendation was given him.

The following are extracts from notices of Mr. Aldridge's acting, which have appeared in different newspapers upon this his latest appearance before a London audience :—

From the MORNING POST, March 21, 1848 :

Mr. Ira Aldridge is a *bonâ fide* African, of mulatto tint, with woolly hair; his features are capable of much expression, his action is unrestrained and picturesque, and his voice clear, full, and resonant. It was interesting to witness the acting of Mr. Ira Aldridge, a native of Africa, giving utterance to the wrongs of his race in his assumed character, and standing in an attitude of triumph over the body of one of its oppressors. Mr. Ira Aldridge is an intelligent actor, and his elocutionary powers are admirable. Compared with the people by whom he was last night surrounded, he might with strict justice be considered a true Roscius.

From the MORNING HERALD, of March 22, 1848 :

A mulatto, of the name of Aldridge, appeared on Monday night at the Surrey Theatre, in the character of Zanga, meeting with all the success which cleverness and considerable experience would be likely to ensure. Mr. Aldridge is evidently a man of intelligence, and his personation of the revengeful hero of Young's disagreeable tragedy was discriminative, energetic, and disfigured by no clumsinesses or incongruities of elocution. He was loudly applauded; and upon being called before the curtain, propitiated the countenance of the audience in a neat and well-turned address. He afterwards appeared in "The Padlock"—playing the part of Mungo with much drollery.

From the MORNING ADVERTISER, March 21, 1848 :

He achieved complete success, and it is nothing more than justice to his merits to say he deserved it. He has a clear and flexible voice, which he uses with great judgment and taste; he can infuse great expression and feeling into his intonation ; his emphasis is judicious; and his transitions natural and appropriate. His acting was excellent throughout. Without attempting to institute a comparative criticism between the performance or merits of this gentleman and any of those who might be considered to be his competitors, we may venture to say that he stands, without question, in the first class. In the farce of " The Padlock," his performance of the part of Mungo was equal to anything we have ever witnessed, displaying great humour and histrionic art in setting forth the salient points of that very facetious specimen of sable servants. The greatest applause accompanied his efforts. If this gentleman has assigned to him characters equally well calculated to call forth his abilities, he cannot fail to be a great acquisition to the theatre, and to attract good houses, which, after all, is the great desideratum in these cases.

From the LONDON TELEGRAPH, March 29, 1848 :

A native-born African appearing on our Stage is somewhat of a curiosity in histrionic annals ; and it afforded us a pleasing proof of the wearing away of that prejudice against men of a colour different from our own, which has long lurked in the hearts of nearly all of us, that Mr. Aldridge, the " African Roscius," who on Monday night performed the part of Othello at this theatre, was, by a numerous and respectable audience, most favourably received. Mr. Aldridge's impersonation of the brave man who loved "not wisely but too well," is a treat of a high order. With the similitude of country and complexion, the illusion becomes exceedingly strong, whilst the critic has not to object to a defective knowledge of the language in which our great dramatist originally introduced this splendid conception. In the expression of love, rage, jealousy, and despair, this performance presented the skill of a consummate knowledge of the human passions, wrought, as it were, to a powerful and fearful reality. From the first moment in which the poison of jealousy taints his heart, till the " green-eyed monster" marked him for its own, in the progress of the passion, its deep workings, until he raged in the convulsions of agonising thoughts and convictions, the interest never flagged for a moment. Some passages merit the warmest praise, amongst which we may select the pathetic reference to his personal disadvantages. The scene in which Iago first attempts to excite his jealousy, when as yet " He doubts—yet doats—suspects, yet strongly loves," and the solemn impressiveness with which he declares, " I had rather be a toad and live upon the vapour of a dungeon, &c."

There was no clap-tap, no rant, even in the most vigorous and impassioned scenes; but truth to nature, and a just conception of character, were evidenced throughout.

From the SUNDAY TIMES, March 26, 1848:

His delineation of the proud, revengeful Moor was finely conceived, and executed with great dramatic effect. In the soliloquies, and those passages in which the reflective powers of the mind are at work, while the material action is suspended, he possesses the rare faculty of completely abstracting and separating himself from all external objects, or of only receiving impressions from those that harmonise with the state of his mind. Zanga's opening soliloquy in the first act, during the storm, expresses this mental condition very forcibly. In scenes of emotion Mr. Aldridge is exceedingly natural; his grief and joy seem to spring directly from his heart, and have a contagious influence upon his audience. Nothing could have been more admirably pourtrayed than the exultation of Zanga when he finds that his schemes for the destruction of Alonzo are ripening to success. There is a mad intoxication in his joy—an intensity in his savage delight that is scarcely less terrible than his rage. Of the better feelings of our nature we have but few indications in the character of the Moor brooding over his long-cherished vengeance; occasionally, however, we have touches of humanity gleaming athwart the dark picture, which were elicited with great effect by Mr. Aldridge. The remembrance of his father's death and his country's wrongs, and his own degradation, which had burned into his heart, is obliterated when he beholds his enemy lifeless at his feet, and the late remorse of a noble heart was expressed with deep feeling and pathos, when he exclaims—

" And art thou dead ? So is my enmity—
I war not with the dust."

As regards his general delineation of the Moor's character, it was marked by careful study and judicious conception. Mr. Aldridge played the part of the Negro servant with extraordinary humour and natural drollery. The child-like simplicity of the Negro character—easily excited to mirth or sorrow—with its love of fun and mischief, were admirably pourtrayed by him.

From the DISPATCH, March 26, 1848:

Mr. Ira Aldridge, a gentleman of colour, appeared last week as Zanga, in "The Revenge," and deservedly met with warm encouragement. He is an actor of talent; and in such characters as Zanga can make a very deep impression. He has power to present, in strong, broad, effective bearing, the injuries, sufferings, and passions of the much-abused African. In a totally different character, that of Mungo, in " The Padlock," seldom, or ever, played by a native of the torrid zone, he displayed considerable *vis comica*.

BELL'S LIFE IN LONDON, of March 26, 1848, writes, it will be seen, in *precisely the same words* as the MORNING ADVERTISER of the 21st:

Mr. Ira Aldridge has a clear and flexible voice, which he uses with great judgment and taste; he can infuse great expression and feeling into his intonation;

his emphasis is judicious; and his transitions natural and appropriate. His acting was excellent throughout. Without attempting to institute a comparative criticism between the performance or merits of this gentleman and any of those who might be considered to be his competitors, we may venture to say that he stands, without question, in the first class. In the farce of "The Padlock," his performance of the part of Mungo was equal to anything we ever witnessed, displaying great humour and histrionic art in setting forth the salient points of that very facetious specimen of sable servants. The greatest applause accompanied his efforts. If this gentleman has assigned to him characters equally well calculated to call forth his abilities, he cannot fail to be a great acquisition to the theatre, and to attract good houses, which, after all, is the great desideratum in these cases.

From the WEEKLY TIMES, March 26, 1848:

Mr. Ira Aldridge is a *bonâ fide* African, of mulatto tint, with woolly hair; his features are capable of much expression, his action is unrestrained and picturesque, and his voice clear, full, and resonant. His powers of energetic declamation are very marked, and the whole of his acting appears impulsed by a current of feeling of no inconsiderable weight and vigour, yet controlled and guided in a manner that clearly shows the actor to be a person of much study and great Stage experience.

From the OBSERVER, March 26, 1848:

Mr. Aldridge has a clear and flexible voice, which he uses with great judgment and taste; he knows how to infuse considerable expression and feeling into his intonation; his emphasis is judicious; and his transitions were natural and appropriate. Without attempting to institute a comparative criticism between the performance or merits of this gentleman and any of those who might be considered to be his competitors, we may venture to say that he stands, without question, in a high class. In the farce of "The Padlock," his performance of the part of Mungo was excellent, displaying great humour and histrionic art in setting forth the salient points of that very facetious specimen of sable servants.

From the ERA, March 26, 1848:

On Monday (March 20, 1848), Mr. Aldridge, "The African Roscius," who has gained a great celebrity in the provinces, appeared at this house in the opposite characters of Zanga, in Young's tragedy of "The Revenge," and Mungo, in the farce of "The Padlock." This was not Mr. Aldridge's first bow to a London audience. Some years ago, he performed two nights running as Othello, at Covent Garden, and afterwards went through several parts at the Surrey. He was at that time very young, and has since, by continual practice, improved himself in every respect as an actor. He was, however, highly successful when he last appeared in London. The papers spoke of his performance in terms of unequivocal commendation; but, notwithstanding the novelty of a man of colour representing Shakspere's intellectual heroes so as to meet the serious approval of critics, and the extraordinary circumstance of Mr. Aldridge (although a black) taking his stand in the profession as a gentleman and a scholar, capable of receiving the poet's creations, and pourtraying his thoughts in a display of histrionic art—notwithstanding the general approval he met with, and the encouragement he ought to have received, he made but little way as an actor of great pretensions, and soon disappeared from the London boards. Ridicule had something to do with this. The disadvantage of colour, which excluded him from all chance of success in America, was not entirely overcome in England among a prejudiced, wanton, and unthinking few, who could not let an opportunity pass for sneering at and ridiculing the "presumptuous nigger." One publication in particular, now out of print, was particularly unmerciful, and its lampoons were sadly discouraging to the tenacious young "Roscius," for ridicule does not always blunt the feelings of those against whom it is directed, but, on the contrary, often makes them more susceptible. Mr. Aldridge, however, is, in our opinion, likely to outlive such petty attacks as he was then subjected to. His appearance at the Surrey has been promising in the extreme, and we think his London engagements this time will be both gratifying and profitable to him. He is a very excellent actor. Like all of his race, and his country itself, he is one of extremes. The earnestness of seriousness is equal to the heartiness of his mirth. As Zanga he is exceedingly fine, looking the character of the Moor to perfection, and acting it with great power and correctness. For the tragedy itself we have little regard. It was written when mere declamation was admired, and the College critic sat in the pit to applaud stilted language, which is now looked upon as so much grammatical nonsense. Still there are some stirring passages in "The Revenge," and some melodramatic situations, and of these Mr. Aldridge avails himself very effectively. It was interesting to mark the subdued tone and superior acting of the African, as compared with the wild and unmeaning rant of those who "supported" him. In his passionate deliveries he received much applause, and upon those occasions his voice rises to ringing, clear, and distinct accents, while at others he speaks in a measured and grave style, almost too sober to be in keeping with the fiery nature of the Moor. We look upon him as an extraordinary personage, and quite a curiosity to those who take any interest in the physiology of man. In farce he is exceedingly funny. You see the veritable nigger, whose good-nature, humour, and even wit, are so commonly ridiculed. As Mungo he is very amusing, giving way to his absurdity with all the zest of one of his colour. Mr. Aldridge sings, too, and his "Possum up a Gum-tree" is one of the funniest things that can be imagined. No mock "Ethiopian Serenader" could come near it. It is novel to see one who has been obtaining much applause in pourtraying passion in its most poetic shape, descend to the broad farce of mock drunkenness, and cramming into his capacious mouth a lighted candle, which he mistakes for the neck of a bottle in the other hand; and it is only a man of natural genius who can do both so as to be commended for the faithfulness of his mimicry. On Monday next, Mr. Aldridge will appear as Othello, a character for which he is so peculiarly fitted. We are inclined to believe that he will be very attractive as the "darky husband" of the fair Desdemona. We advise the anti-slavery people, who visit Exeter Hall upon great occasions, to see Mr. Aldridge at the Surrey. His appearance there is a "great moral lesson" in favour of anti-slavery.

Again, on April 8, 1848, the ERA says:

There is a repose, a dignity, and a natural gravity and earnestness about Mr. Aldridge's personification of the dusky Moor that are particularly impressive. He is very fine in the part, and the natural hue of his skin helps to make the illusion perfect. There is much originality, too, about the African's delineation of the character. His declamation has all the dignity, and his action all the grace, which belong to primitive races. Nor is he wanting in that refinement without which there is but little to admire in man, as he appears before the more civilized of his species. Mr. Aldridge is something more than an African: he is a scholar and a gentleman; at least, he acts like one. In Othello, he delivers the most difficult passages with a degree of correctness that surprises the beholder, and, at times, he ascends to a pourtrayal of the conflicting passions of the jealous husband in a manner both artistical and true. The workings of his mind, and sensations of his heart, were conspicuous in his swarthy visage, and depicted in every gesture. After the death of Desdemona, when he awoke to a consciousness of the deception that had been practised upon him, in the frenzy of his remorse he lifted the lifeless body of his murdered and wronged wife from the bed, as though she had been an infant. There was something terribly touching in this display of physical strength, wrought up by mental agony.

From the ILLUSTRATED LONDON NEWS (with an engraving of the African Roscius as Zanga, in "The Revenge"):

Mr. Aldridge possesses an excellent voice, commanding figure, and expressive countenance; to which he adds the advantages of education and study. His dress, which is novel and picturesque, reminds one of the portraits of Abd-el-Kader. Throughout the play he more than realized the high encomiums that had previously been passed upon him; and many who ridiculed the idea of a native-born African successfully representing a dramatic character, retired with very different feelings. Nor is his talent confined to tragedy. His representation of Mungo, in "The Padlock," is a laughable performance, differing entirely from the Ethiopian absurdities we have been taught to look upon as correct portraitures; his total *abandon* is very amusing. He re-appeared on the 27th as Othello, with great success.

From DOUGLAS JERROLD'S NEWSPAPER, of March 25, 1848:

On Monday, Mr. Aldridge, a Negro, performed the part of Zanga, and although the selection of such an individual looked like the parading a piece of reality, by having a real black man to represent the ideal character, and, therefore, seemed to be an insufferable piece of vulgarity, yet we thought it our duty to witness it. We were agreeably disappointed. Mr. Aldridge is an undoubted Negro, but is gifted with an intelligence of perception, dignity of action, and force of expression, that not only do honour to his particular race, but to humanity. He reads with much feeling and appreciation of the author; and there is a force and vigour in his passionate enunciation that is stirring, and perfectly free from imitation or rant. He especially possesses a freedom of gait and natural dignity of movement, derivable probably from the unconfined nature of his early life. He has nothing of the savage, but his freedom from the petty manners of conventional training. He made as much of Zanga as it is possible to do of so wordy, blustering, aud clumsy an Iago. He has a slight foreign accent, and his voice, like most of his countrymen, is thin in the upper tones. He immediately afterwards performed Mungo, in "The Padlock," and with so much humour, and with such characteristic songs, that it gave universal satisfaction, and it is doubtful whether his *forte* be not rather comedy than tragedy. It is certain he is a man of no mean amount of talent, and its range is considerable, as is proved by his clever delineation alike of Zanga and Mungo. He was enthusiastically received by a very excellent house, and we are quite sure his complexion will be no impediment to his receiving the applause due to his merit.

The SATIRIST, of April 2, 1848, says:

The African Roscius continues to draw good houses at the Surrey, from the novelty of seeing "a real black," and the more especially a tragic actor, which Mr. Aldridge is, beyond all doubt. His Othello is a very superior piece of acting, well considered, and well developed; the latter part, where, after the death of Desdemona, he becomes conscious of her innocence, his desperation, and the abandoning of himself to the furies of his mind, were touches of the highest excellence. As an actor he has fought his way through every opposition and prejudice, and as a foreigner and a stranger comes to England to delineate the poetic conceptions of England's bard.

Other London papers speak of Mr. Aldridge in similar terms. Upon the principle of "what everybody says must be true," Mr. Aldridge must be a man of no ordinary talent. As a whole his performances are, according to every testimony that has been given in reference to them, extraordinarily fine, whatever may be the occasional objections that spring up in the minds of those who endeavour to find faults in them. He is, however, before a public who will judge for themselves; that they admire his efforts is very evident in the encouragement he receives, and that his various and peculiar merits may be more generally known and tested, this brief history of his life and labours has been written.

The African, notwithstanding all that has been said of him, has yet to be brought fairly and completely before the London public, by whom he is, comparatively speaking, unknown. His engagement at the Surrey Theatre has just terminated with offers to renew it; but it is on the Middlesex side the water he must take his stand and be thoroughly tested. PUNCH, seeing a joke and availing himself of it, said lately:—

"IRA EST FUROR BREVIS."—The theatrical critics are loud in praise of a real Ethiopian tragedian, a Mr. Aldridge, with the unusual Christian name of *Ira*, which is, no doubt, symbolical of its owner being "the rage," wherever he goes.

Mr. Aldridge will, no doubt, soon come forward more conspicuously than he has hitherto done, and justify the above remark. At Edinburgh, Mr. W. Murray, the spirited manager of the Theatre Royal, took great pleasure in helping to his successes, while the Scotch people have shown a marked appreciation of his merits. Such has been precisely the case with Mr. Calcraft and the Irish; facts to which Mr. Aldridge refers with lively and mingled sentiments of pride and gratitude.

We have witnessed the performances of Mr. Aldridge, and if testimony to his superior abilities and accomplishments as a tragic and comic actor were wanting, we would readily add our own humble opinion of them. But those qualities are beyond dispute. He possesses every mental and physical requisite for such parts as he fills, and is an ornament to his profession, and a credit, not only to his race in particular, but to society at large, of which he is a bright, albeit a jetty member. In the character of Othello—his special favourite (for he has a decided preference for serious parts)—he seems to have precisely Dr. Johnson's conception of it. That great critic says :—" The fiery openness of Othello, magnanimous, artless, and credulous, boundless in confidence, ardent in his affection, inflexible in his resolution, and obdurate in his revenge, are proofs of Shakspeare's skill in human nature." Mr. Aldridge feels and acts all this.

In " The Slave," he is solemn in the intensity of his hatred, bursting out occasionally into a blaze of fierce invective and passionate declamation, and then hiding the fire of his feelings beneath the assumed servility necessary to his purpose and his station. There is no other actor who exhibits the same amount of gravity, save Mr. Macready, who carries his seriousness, to our humble thinking, to an unnatural extreme. Mr. Macready puts on the "intense earnestness" and " wrapped fixedness" which belong to greatness of soul, and wears the garments well; but they are evidently borrowed for the occasion, however much they become the wearer, and exhibit his skill in the adjustment of each particular fold. Mr. Aldridge, on the other hand, appears in such robes as though they fell upon him without an effort to possess them, and he wears, as it were, his own by right of inheritance. The dark shades of his face become doubly sombre in their thoughtful aspect; there is something true to nature in the nightlike gloom that is spread over them; an expression more terrible than paler lineaments can assume.

In farce, Mr. Aldridge is funny, as he is serious in tragedy. The ebony becomes polished—the coal emits sparks. His face is the faithful index of his mind, and as there is not a darker frown than his, so is there not a broader grin. The ecstacy of his long shrill note, in " Oppossum up a gum-tree," can only be equalled by the agony of his cry over the body of Desdemona. The sublime and the ridiculous defined, but not blended or confounded one with the other.

With these few general observations upon his acting, we conclude our task—one hastily performed, and shaped out of a handful of loose materials, such as a few old playbills, newspaper notices, and some memoranda that were indispensable. Mr. Aldridge, although aware that a string of such facts as are here set forth, would be calculated to advance his fame and increase public curiosity respecting him, has, with characteristic diffidence, left the entire construction of the narrative to the discretion of the writer, whose comments have been the gratuitous convictions consequent upon the simple facts submitted to him. Should the reader detect what he deems to be remarks too partial, and conclusions one-sided, some allowance, it is hoped, will be made for the bias which the mind naturally receives when engaged upon an undertaking in which its sympathies are excited, and when its approval is justified by the evidence it elicits. We lay down our pen thoroughly persuaded that, even with a set-off thus deducted from the gross amount of favourable construction contained in these pages, Mr. Ira Aldridge, the African Roscius, will, in no respect, be a loser by the interesting truths that remain, and others of his colour may see occasion to rejoice in their publicity.

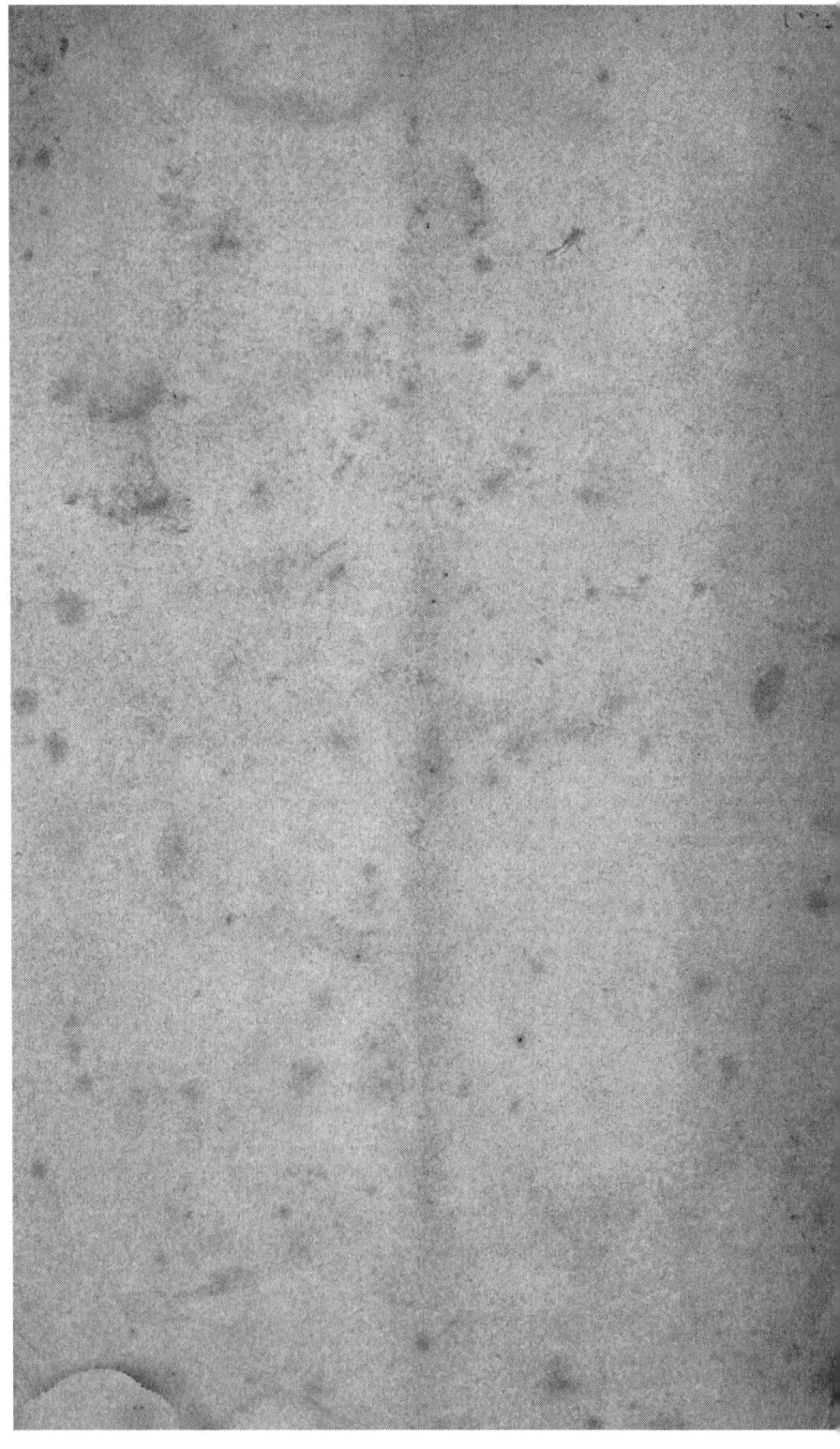